THE ENGLISH GENTLEMAN

THE ENGLISH
GENTLEMAN

Douglas Sutherland

INTRODUCTION BY
SIR IAIN MONCREIFFE OF THAT ILK, BT

DRAWINGS BY
TIMOTHY JAQUES

DEBRETT'S PEERAGE LTD
THE VIKING PRESS · NEW YORK

Text Copyright © Douglas Sutherland 1978
Illustrations Copyright © Timothy Jaques 1978

Published in 1979 by The Viking Press
625 Madison Avenue, New York, NY 10022

Designed and printed by The Compton Press Ltd
The Old Brewery, Tisbury, Wiltshire, England
Library of Congress catalog card number: 78–62997

ISBN 0–670–29681–3

First impression June 1978
Second impression July 1978

Contents

	Foreword	vii
	Introduction *by Sir Iain Moncreiffe of that Ilk, Bt*	ix
1	The Gentleman at Home	1
2	The Gentleman and his School	9
3	The Gentleman and his Club	13
4	The Gentleman and the Opposite Sex	20
5	The Gentleman and his Car	27
6	The Gentleman at Play	31
7	The Gentleman at War	37
8	The Gentleman Abroad	42
9	The Gentleman and his Wardrobe	46
10	The Gentleman and his Relationships	53
11	The Gentleman and the Church	58
12	The Gentleman and his Domestic Habits	60
13	The Gentleman and his Money	65
14	How to be a Gentleman	67

Foreword

EVER since the nineteenth century and long before that for all I know, there has been a regular stream of little books designed to help those who desire to be part of the upper classes. In the past these books have been written by men and women, largely for women, and concerned with such profundities as how to address a Duke or an Archbishop, or what to do with your finger-bowl.

It has always been assumed that the most desirable position in the world is to be accepted as a lady or gentleman. It was assumed by many from Jane Austen to Daphne du Maurier that it is the surest way to happiness and possibly even to eternal salvation.

This book, I hope, is different in that it is the first one to be written by a man, almost exclusively for men. It examines what makes or breaks the gentleman and leaves it to the reader to decide whether he wishes to be part of the upper classes or not. It is also hoped that this volume will be helpful to ladies who wish to be able to recognize the gentleman when they meet one, and to let them know what they are in for should they be reckless enough to marry one.

D.S.

Introduction

DURING the Peasants' Revolt, that most literally revolting peasant, John Ball, asked 'When Adam delved and Eve span, Who then was Gentleman?' The answer is obvious: Adam. How could it have been Eve?

Adam, however, was forced to give up his status of gentleman on expulsion from the Garden of Eden. His descendants have ever since been working to retrieve that position. But the snag is that the idea of openly paid work is itself incompatible with the basic idea of life in that Garden. So the work has to be concealed lest it defeats its own object.

This was to some extent understood by the *noblesse* of France and, I believe, the *adel* of the Holy Roman Empire. The idea there was that a gentleman served the Crown for the common good and did not engage in commerce for his own benefit (except on so grand a scale as to blind the beholder); so he was exempt from the State's ordinary taxation levied on those who did otherwise. In England, there was latent the rather similar idea that those who already had ample private means should tend to serve for nominal pay in the armed forces, the Church or the diplomatic service rather than seek to increase their personal wealth, and that those engaged otherwise shouldn't talk about it. On reflection, nobody doubts that Sir Alec Douglas-Home has worked hard for the country all his life, but nobody classes him as a 'worker' like some spivs we could name. This Scarlet Pimpernel attitude fools the unwary into believing that 'idle' and 'rich' are almost synonymous:

though of course gentlemen aren't supposed to be openly rich. Theirs is the concept of the amateur as opposed to the professional.

We are of course not dealing here at all with the peculiarly *Scottish* concept of the gentleman, which is so linked to clannish pride and probably embraces at least a tenth of those of Scottish, especially Highland, descent. It has been said that you can recognize a highland gentleman by the scurf on his shoes (I won't enter into the Mitford-Ross discussion here except to say that 'dandruff' is definitely Non-U), but there is much more to it than that. As a descendant in the male line of William, Earl of Sutherland in 1235, the author of course falls into the Scottish as well as the English category. But here Major Sutherland is writing about the *English*, and by extension the British, variety.

Of course, birth also enters into the concept of the English gentleman. My grandmother, widowed in India in the reign of the Queen-Empress Victoria, told me a well-known couplet that took a cruel swipe at each of two Molesworths who had just arrived out as sahibs: the one boasting of more ancient lineage than the other.

> There are two *Moles* of equal *worth*.
> But not, it seems, of equal birth.
> The Mole, alas, whose blood is blue,
> Is far the bloodier of the two.

But, with that mobility between classes that so distinguishes England from the Continent, the idea of the gentleman has since the end of the Middle Ages been linked more to a way of life.

The following quotation from *The Observer* of 13 April 1806 illustrates this point.

Singular Conviction: A Curate of a village near town and one of the Overseers of the Parish, a gentleman farmer, had a dispute respecting some private business, and the Farmer d—d the Clergyman's eyes. For this offence he was brought before the Magistrates of Marlborough Street, and convicted in the penalty of 5s. The Farmer contended that he was *not* a gentleman, and that he ought to pay no more than 1s. This objection was over-ruled, as it appeared that he kept his sporting dogs, and took his wine after dinner.

Douglas Sutherland's book therefore is an account of that apparently vanishing species which cheerfully ran a vast chunk of the globe without openly taking work too seriously. Wearing dinner jackets in the jungle when not disguised on secret service to detect t'huggee, they unobtrusively abolished slavery, cannibalism and widow-burning, among other trifles. Foreigners at heart, like the late Harold Laski who wrote *The Danger of Being a Gentleman*, could never begin to understand them. Nor is the species really vanishing – though elusive specimens of the present generation described in this book are nevertheless getting harder for the un-initiated to find outside a few select private zoos called clubs. The coming generation of English leopards are, as usual, and with long practice in camouflage, quietly engaged in adjusting their spots. Meanwhile, this book may serve as a guide to the seeker after initiation.

SIR IAIN MONCREIFFE OF THAT ILK

1

The Gentleman at Home

The Englishman's home is his castle

GENTLEMEN do not usually live in cities. At whatever discomfort to themselves and their families they prefer to live in the country and then only in selected parts of it.

I can well remember a conversation with an elderly friend of mine about a mutual acquaintance whom we both agreed was a bounder. Although there are few worse things that one gentleman can say about another, my friend went further, 'He is not only a bounder,' he declared, 'he is also a liar.' These were strong words indeed. 'What do you think of this?' he asked. 'The fellow told me he had a house in the country and I found out he lived in Surrey.' It was certainly damning evidence.

The truth is that the Home Counties, with their commuter population, housing development schemes and lack of foxes, are no longer suited to the gentleman's way of life. It upsets his peace of mind to observe the hardships inflicted upon his neighbours by unheated trains and railway strikes, although he himself is unaffected by such things. He has quite enough to do at home without fooling around in the City with stocks and shares or running companies for ungrateful shareholders. Gentlemen prefer to live in out of the way places with names like Hogsnorton-in-the-Wold or Blistering-under-Wychwood and grumble about *The Times* being a day late.

Gentlemen live in houses at the end of tree-lined

drives, the surface of which is a trial to the springs of the sturdiest of vehicles. They do not announce the names of their houses at the gate, assuming that anyone they wish to see already knows where they live. There is a back drive for tradesmen on which the going is even rougher but which is suffered by the postman, the garbage collectors and the grocer's delivery boy with philosophical resignation as part of the privilege of serving the 'big house'.

The size of a gentleman's house is in inverse proportion to the distance it is from London. There are, of course, some very large houses indeed quite near London but they have either been opened to the public so that the gentleman and his family are reduced to living in an area not much larger than a council flat or have been converted into houses for the insane. In Ireland and the remoter parts of Scotland many gentlemen live in castles which are so large that even the Commissioners in Lunacy would not consider taking them over.

Inside the Gentleman's Home

What all gentlemen's houses have in common are long dark corridors, windows with inside wooden shutters and a special arrangement whereby the kitchen is situated as far from the dining-room as is architecturally possible. They smell of a mixture of soft soap and cucumber and their inhabitants have learned to live with damp, dry rot and open fireplaces. They sleep in unheated bedrooms with the windows wide open for they are very healthy in early life. In later years, of course, they become crippled with rheumatism.

There are exceptions to this passion for fresh air. One gentleman of my acquaintance had a wholly deplorable preference for a warm bedroom. On being asked to stay in a house known for its arctic temperatures he took the precaution of packing a suitcase full of

coal so that he could light a clandestine fire. Unfortunately, while the butler was struggling up the circular staircase the suitcase burst open and the contents rolled all the way down into the hall.

Gentlemen do not buy furniture. They inherit it. The last time any furniture was bought by gentlemanly families was in the Victorian era with the result that their drawing-rooms are still filled with understuffed sofas, high-backed chairs and little tables which fall over when you put anything on them. Equally, gentlemen never throw anything away, so that when a piece of furniture finally collapses, another is dusted off and taken down from the attic. This is quite likely to be a survival from the Regency, so gentlemen's houses are becoming steadily better furnished as time goes on, rather than the other way round. This applies as much to poor gentlemen who are struggling to make ends meet as to gentlemen who are comfortably off. The only way the uninitiated can tell if a gentleman is rich or poor is that in poor gentlemen's houses the brass doorknobs are apt to come off in your hand.

It is obligatory for gentlemen to know who their ancestors were and to hang their pictures on the walls to prove it. This is a great embarrassment to parvenu 'gentlemen' who have to spend a great deal of time acquiring other people's ancestors from special shops run by other parvenu 'gentlemen' who supply restored and reframed 'instant ancestors' even down to bogus name plates. This results in a great many more Gainsboroughs, Lelys, Reynolds and Lawrences being in existence than those artists ever had time to paint.

Gentleman also like to hoard relics of the great days of the British Empire – assegais from the Matabele campaign, daggers from China and a solar topee with a hole in the brim where great-uncle George tried to shoot himself in Pondicherry and missed.

Plumbing Arrangements

There is no room in the house which better demon-
strates the gentleman's preoccupation with living in
the past than his bathroom. The marbled magnificences
with gold taps so beloved by Hollywood film stars are
not for him. He sticks resolutely to the high narrow
baths of his forebears which have brown marks on the
enamel caused by years of dripping taps and the lavatories are enclosed in a mahogany box where you pull
the handle upwards to flush. The bowls of gentlemen's
lavatories always have the name of the maker boldly
engraved in the china, an innocent vanity on the part
of Victorian lavatory makers which has regrettably now
fallen into disuse. The name carrying the most prestige
on a gentleman's lavatory is that of Thomas Crapper,
because Mr Crapper for many years had the honour of
making loos for the Royal Family. For reasons of deli-
cacy, however, he was not allowed to emblazon his wares
with the Royal coat of arms. A Crapper crapper has
nonetheless much the same *cachet* today as a pair of
Purdey shotguns.

Other Rooms

There are certain rooms in a gentleman's house which
are not found in those of more ordinary mortals. One
is the Morning Room where the daily papers are laid
out to keep company with back issues of *The Field*, the
Country Gentleman's Association Magazine and last
year's copy of the Army and Navy Stores catalogue.
There is also a desk with clean blotting paper, pens
with Waverley nibs and writing paper embossed with
the name of the nearest railway station and not only
with the telephone number but the telegraphic address.
Gentlemen do not on the whole trust the telephone.

Another very gentlemanly room is the billiards room

[5]

although billiards is no longer played there since the game has been taken up by the lower classes. Besides which, the cues have long since lost their tips and become warped with damp. The billiards room, in houses which do not boast a separate library, is often lined with books which by family tradition are very valuable and are kept behind locked glass doors to which the key has long since been lost. Gentleman are not, generally speaking, great readers, confining their attention to the *Bloodstock Yearbook, Burke's Landed Gentry* and *Debrett*. The main function of the billiards room is as a sort of adult rumpus room where the menfolk repair after a good dinner to play a game known as billiard fives which involves hitting the ball with the flat of the hand. It is extremely painful if played enthusiastically and is thirsty work. The billiards table also provides a convenient place for gentlemen to sleep under when overcome with the evening's jollifications.

Nannies

Because gentlemen have been largely reared by their nannies they develop an attachment for them which remains undimmed with the passing of the years. Nannies never retire but continue to live, long after their charges have married and had children of their own, in 'nanny's room'. There they sit all day long, surrounded by eyeless teddy bears and broken toys, knitting endless pairs of socks and sewing on trouser buttons. Gentlemen visit their nannies every morning to assure them that they have been to the lavatory and have brushed their teeth. Gentlemen's wives do not get on very well with gentlemen's nannies, considering them proper old humbugs Gentlemen's wives are usually in the right about this.

Domestic Quarters

A notable feature of gentlemen's houses is the number of rooms which have fallen into disuse with the passing of the army of servants who used to be essential to their comfort. In extreme cases gentlemen have even pulled down complete wings without noticeably diminishing the amount of surplus accommodation such as laundry rooms, servants' halls, housekeepers' rooms and butlers' pantries. There are also endless maids' bedrooms still furnished with iron bedsteads and linoleumed floors and with iron bars across the windows designed to prevent the more romantically minded from climbing out after dark to keep assignations in the bushes with passionate gardeners' boys. As a further aid to virtue there are often improving texts hung on the bare walls, bearing such valuable advice as 'Sleep not for ye know not when the Master cometh'.

On the whole, gentlemen's houses are not very comfortable places to live in by comparison with what those lower down the social scale are permitted to enjoy.

2

The Gentleman and his School

Manners makyth Man
WINCHESTER COLLEGE MOTTO

Schoolmasters

MASTERS at gentlemanly schools are a race apart. They wear their gowns in a particular way, walk in a particular way, talk in a particular way and are united in the belief that all their charges will come to a sticky end. They spend most of their time peeping round corners to discover if somebody is having a furtive drag at a cigarette or engaged in even more reprehensible practices.

Whilst most masters have very suspicious natures, others are benign to a point of naïvety.

A friend of mine was being shown around a very distinguished school by the headmaster when he was taken short and asked if he could use the boys' lavatories. The headmaster, who prided himself on his liberal attitudes, gave his permission but warned him not to be shocked at anything he might see scrawled on the lavatory walls. Filled with curiosity, my friend conducted a fruitless search in each of the compartments. He was just giving up when he discovered, etched with a nail file high up on one of the walls, the scandalous words 'Down with Harrow'.

While on the subject of schoolmasters it is only fair to add that many, particularly at the more aristocratic schools, are positively eccentric. They are generally regarded with tolerant affection by their pupils which may explain why gentlemen, in later life, so readily accept the eccentricity of many of their peers.

A good example of pedagogic eccentricity is the experience of the mother of a boy who had asked to see his housemaster and was shown into a drawing room where a gentleman was seated behind a newspaper. After a considerable wait she plucked up the courage to ask her companion if he was also waiting to see Dr J—. Slowly lowering the paper, the man said, 'I *am* Dr J—'.

The Virtue of Sports

The rich man who would send his son to a gentleman's school would be less than realistic if he were to examine their rival merits in terms of scholastic achievement. The only criterion is what games they play. In bald terms the choice is between the soccer schools and the rugby schools. Rugby schools tend to look down on soccer schools and soccer schools have an inferiority complex because none of their pupils go on to play for Arsenal or Liverpool. Eton, which is a soccer school, are dreadful show-offs because they have a game of their own called the Wall Game at which nobody has scored a goal within living memory. Gentlemen from rugby schools sometimes go on to become internationals but this is because few people in their right minds play the game unless they are gentlemen, particularly those of Scottish, Irish or Welsh origin who want to assert their minority rights.

The greatest fear that gentlemen suffer when they send their sons to gentlemanly schools is that they will not live up to the traditions with which they themselves were indoctrinated. To play for the first eleven, to win the cross-country run or to have whacked more boys than any of their contemporaries are all laudable achievements.

In former days failure to conform to the public school system would have resulted in the offender being sent to the Colonies to work out his destiny. Some parents who were disappointed in their sons even sent them to work in city offices like merchant bankers and did not mention their names again until they became chairmen of public companies.

It would be unrealistic, however, to suggest that to send one's son to a public school today still carries the same *cachet* as it did up to the beginning of the last war.

Indeed, there are some gentlemen nowadays who do not send their sons to public schools at all but send them to schools where their education is paid for by the State. This perversity is not, however, the result of the awakening of a new democratic spirit among the upper classes but as a result of a realistic talk with their bank managers who convince them that, the price of whisky and cartridges being what they are, to do so would be seriously to jeopardize their own standard of life.

At the same time there are a large number of boys who are sent to public schools these days who would have found it difficult to gain entry in the days when headmasters could afford to be more discriminating about the parents' social backgrounds. I can remember in my time an unfortunate boy, whose father had made a vast fortune in scrap metal, who, whenever the local junk lorry pulled into the quadrangle, would be greeted with cries of: 'Hurry along there, Jones Minor. Your Dad has just arrived.'

Another father, who had made a great deal of money in cattle dealing, thought it diplomatic to describe himself as a stockbroker when entering his son for Eton.

Whilst the traditional gentleman's school has perhaps become more democratic, it has also become more socially sensitive.

Not so long ago any boy who, perhaps as a result, many generations back, of an indiscretion by an empire-building ancestor, had a slightly swarthy complexion, would invariably be nicknamed 'Nigger' and no more was thought about the matter. Nowadays even the most gentlemanly schools have numbers of pupils from foreign parts whose parents would take great objection to such a distinction and would probably complain to the Race Relations Board.

This emancipation, however, does have the advantage for the gentleman's son on leaving school of no longer being viewed with such suspicion by potential employers if he applies for a job as a bus conductor or a policeman.

3

The Gentleman and his Club

There is nowhere more felicitous than a seat in a good club
DR JOHNSON

ALL GENTLEMEN belong to a good club. They do so
for a number of reasons, many of which are unconnec-
ted with what an outsider might consider to be a club's
main purpose – a sociable meeting place. In fact, clubs
are very often not sociable places at all. For example,
there was the case of the elderly member of one of the
most exclusive of all clubs who complained most bit-
terly to the Secretary: 'D'ye know,' he said, 'there was a
demned young fellow I have never met, who came up to
me in the hall and said "Good morning"!' 'Good gracious,' said the Secretary, who must be all things to all
members, 'whatever did you say?' 'Well', said the old
member reasonably enough, 'I did not want to appear
rude so I just turned me back and walked away.'

Another reason for a gentleman joining a club may
be because his father and his grandfather belonged to
it before him. More likely it is because he finds it a
convenient place to have parcels sent or messages taken
or for the equally practical reason that it is the one
place where he is not expected to tip.

Difficulty of Election
The qualifications for joining a club are that the candidate's presence should not be offensive to anybody already in the club – however cantankerous the existing
members might be. For this purpose the best clubs have

retained the old system of 'blackballing' a candidate. This means that the members of the election committee are each armed with a black ball and a white ball. If any member drops a black ball into the ballot box, the candidate is turned down. Members who are not on the election committee can, of course, influence those who are and in this way many old scores are paid off. A boy who filches another boy's tuck at school had better beware lest he finds his victim in later life belonging to a club he desires to join.

Great wealth made in the lifetime of a candidate is a definite disadvantage when his election to a good club is considered. There was at least one exceptionally rich self-made man whose last and remaining ambition was to join an exclusive club. To achieve this end, and knowing the perils of the black ball, he managed to bribe a popular but impecunious member to do some lobbying on his behalf. The man worked assiduously for many months so that when the day of the election arrived there was a certain amount of confidence in the tycoon's camp. However, when the box was opened it held so many black balls that the contents resembled nothing more than a giant helping of caviare. The backwoodsmen who seldom visited the club had rallied to repel the invader.

Another very real difficulty facing the aspirant for membership to an exclusive club is that it is positively bad form to ask a friend to put his name forward. The guest who seeks to flatter his host by saying something like: 'I say, this is a very nice place. I might even consider joining if you wanted to put up my name,' is committing a grave social error. He must wait to be invited. There are many reasons why a gentleman might wish to decline to put forward a candidate, not the least being that in many clubs he himself would feel obliged to resign if his candidate was rejected. Many members

of clubs have over the years made themselves so un-
popular that it is not a risk they would care to run.

Exclusivity

Of course there are several well-known clubs which can
no longer be regarded as exclusive. Some have become
so desperate for members that they allow members of
the Civil Service to join, which means that you can find
'your obedient servant' drinking next to you at the bar.
Some clubs are so dead in their traditions that they
allow in people who openly earn their own livings and
at least one club allows in 'journalists'. However, even
in these permissive days, the unbreakable rule is that
business of any sort must not be discussed in any form.
Cabinet secrets may be bandied about with the utmost
indiscretion but if any one member were to approach
another about his insurance problems he would be
courting instant expulsion. The best clubs for a gentleman to join are in St James's Street, for many of the
great palaces which line Pall Mall are regarded with
condescension by the more exclusive. One which is a
club for motorists is generally known as 'The Chauf-
feurs' Arms' and another which has many Bishops as
members is known as 'The Clergyman's Rest'. When the
Conservative Club merged with the Bath, it immediately became known to the irreverent as the 'Lava Tory'.
Even among the upper crust of clubs there is a certain
amount of rivalry as to their status. As one member of
a very grand club remarked condescendingly about the
members of another very grand club: 'Their members
back the horses which our members own.'

Privacy

Perhaps the most valuable service which a club offers to
a gentleman is privacy. Once a gentleman walks through
the hallowed portals of his club he cuts himself off from

the outside world and is protected from it by the best hall porters in the world. Creditors have no chance of bearding the clubman in his den and even anxious wives find the greatest difficulty in discovering whether their husbands are lying drunk in the Morning Room.

Club Servants

Club porters have a proprietorial pride in their members which extends into their private lives. A friend of a club member who knew that he could always find him in at a certain time in the evening called to see him. 'He's not here,' the porter told him, adding sorrowfully, 'I'm afraid Mr So-and-so's habits have not been at all regular since he got married.'

The affection which club servants have for their members is not, on the surface, returned in equal measure. There was the elderly servant who was found in tears by the Club Secretary, who asked him what on earth was the matter. 'It's that new member,' he blubbered. 'He "thanked" me for bringing him his coffee. It's the first time I've been thanked in thirty years.'

Don't call us

A particularly devious trick practised by clubmen is to have the name of their club put on their visiting cards instead of giving their home address. This has the same effect as the time-honoured brush-off used in theatrical circles of 'Don't you call us. We'll call you.'

Complaints

Every club has a complaints book where gentlemen can air their grievances. Thus one gentleman may complain that another snores too loudly in the smoking room or consistently fails to raise the lavatory seat. A gentleman of my acquaintance resigned in a huff when three of his fellow members complained that he was helping himself too liberally to the rice pudding.

The Changing Face

Most of the traditional clubs have changed little with the passing of the years largely because of the innate conservatism of the members. Many years ago there was a great brouhaha when the Athenaeum went so far as to install a lift to enable the more elderly to use the facilities of the club above ground level. Unfortunately the proportions of the new lift were almost exactly as if it had been designed to accommodate a coffin standing on end, which enabled the younger members to remark that its real purpose was to facilitate the removal of such ancient members as had died in the bedrooms.

(Incidentally it was the Athenaeum where the late Lord Birkenhead used to stop off to relieve himself on his daily walk from his home to the House of Lords. When challenged, after adopting this practice for some time, as to whether he was a member, he was supposed to have exclaimed: 'Good God, is this place a club as well?')

There are now, however, signs in some of the less distinguished clubs that the conservatism and carefully erected barriers are slowly being broken down. Some clubs in an effort to increase their revenue have even allowed clubmen to bring their wives or lady friends to dine in certain remote rooms on specified nights of the week. As, as someone has rightly remarked, most clubs have the atmosphere of a Duke's house with the Duke lying dead upstairs, it is not a move which has been unanimously approved of by the ladies, who prefer a little more glitter on their evenings out. To add to their discomfort the premises set aside for the use of ladies are often adapted from some remote and unused billiards room or, certainly in one case, an over-large lavatory, which makes the ladies' attitude even more understandable.

[17]

The advantages which gentlemen's clubs used to have in such matters, for example, as members being able to drink and gamble long after establishments open to the general public were closed for the night have largely been eroded by the changing laws which have resulted in a rash of late night rendezvous to which membership is open to almost anyone who cares to apply.

This may be part of the cause for the recent concern amongst gentlemen's clubs over falling membership. Traditionally they have always been more concerned with whom they should exclude rather than with whom they should admit. Now, as many are cautiously opening the doors wider, they are finding with some chagrin that there are not queues of would-be gentlemen clamouring for admission. Just the same, there are still enough good clubs where gentlemen who wish to preserve the traditional barriers can do so and where it is still advisable for a member to put his son's name down at birth. In these the port still circulates after dinner and members can amuse themselves, as one of them once put it, by sitting at the window and 'watching the demned people getting wet outside'.

4
The Gentleman and the Opposite Sex

Gentlemen prefer Blondes
ANITA LOOS

UNLIKE the under-privileged classes gentlemen are not exposed to members of the opposite sex during their formative years. Instead they are sent straight from their nanny's knee to monastic establishments where the only visible female is likely to be a ferocius matron surrounded by rolls of sticking plaster and bottles of cascara evacuant.

During the school holidays they may come in contact with elderly aunts who are acceptable for the donations they occasionally produce from their capacious handbags but who are scarcely likely to produce the first flickerings of desire. If young gentlemen have sisters, they keep the matter a deadly secret and die with embarrassment if they are brought to visit them at half term. Girls as a class are considered sloppy and the young gentleman's admiration is very properly reserved for the captain of games.

It is only fair to add that the same strictures are imposed on upper-class young ladies, whose adolescent passions are confined to their gym mistresses or their horses.

Sexual Education

This is not to say that a young gentleman's education in matters of sex is entirely neglected. His mother may mutter on about the birds and the bees but who wants to listen to all that rot when he can watch his pet guinea pigs in action any day of the week? It is just that he cannot quite visualize himself doing the same thing and he secretly rather hopes that babies really are born under gooseberry bushes.

The result is that most young gentlemen start out in life regarding all females with considerable suspicion.

Inevitably there comes the time when the young ladies and gentlemen are forced into each others' arms at those strange upper-class fertility rites known as debutante dances and it is hard to say which sex is the more embarrassed. The boys assert their manhood by throwing bread rolls, drinking too much champagne and being sick in the bushes while the girls defy their anxious and ambitious parents by running off with any unsuitable bounder who has somehow managed to gatecrash the party.

In more spacious days indulgent fathers used to have their sons instructed in the facts of life by introducing them to one of the many houses in London run by Madams who, so legend went, had hearts of gold. Nowadays, however, professional ladies find it more lucrative and less exhausting to devote themselves to comforting out-of-town businessmen, and young gentlemen find themselves relegated to the amateur league which operates around the coffee bars of the King's Road, Chelsea. The enthusiastic free-for-all which has resulted has made London the envy of her continental neighbours.

Marriage

There does still, however, exist what is generally known as 'The List' and although The Queen has long since washed her hands of the whole business of having young ladies presented at Court, there are still ambitious mums, supported by sycophantic gossip columnists, who persist in perpetuating 'The Season' when young ladies are said to 'come out'.

In days gone by everyone who was anyone socially already knew one another but today this is not the case, so 'The List' is of vital importance. Prepared by a gossip columnist of long standing, it is circulated to mothers of eligible daughters and provides the names of young men who are considered by birth and wealth to be suitable escorts. Not to be included on 'The List' is social disaster. Many a young man so listed is able to give up gainful employment and live off the lavish champagne suppers provided by anxious hostesses almost every night of the season, augmenting his diet with the odd chicken leg concealed in his hip pocket for luncheon the next day.

Gentlemen tend to take less and less part in this ritual and those who do are generally relieved when Goodwood Races, held at the end of July at the Duke of Richmond's private racecourse, officially marks the end of the Season and they are at liberty to make arrangements to move to their shooting lodges in Scotland for the opening of the grouse shooting season on the 12th August, which is much more to their taste.

Gentlemen are also relieved to find that nowadays it is quite permissible for their daughters to take gainful employment, although this does not in their opinion excuse them from the responsibility of eventually marrying suitably – preferably to a young man who has prospects of inheriting an estate where he is able to ask his father-in-law to shoot.

Gentlemen's sons also have this responsibility to an even greater extent. There has never been a time in the history of the upper classes when it has not been expected of the eldest son to marry a lady of fortune, even if it entails the sacrifice of extreme beauty and it is this practical attitude which has enabled many noble houses

to be handed down from generation to generation to
this day.

Postmarital Attitudes

Once a gentleman is married he devotes himself with
commendable energy to the all-important matter of pro-
ducing an heir but, however happy gentlemen's mar-
riages are, they could never be described as wildly
romantic. The honeymoon is more likely to be spent
shooting polar bear in Greenland than splashing in the
sun-kissed waters of the Mediterranean. Nor is the
gentleman fluent with such terms of endearment as
'Darling', 'Sweetheart', or 'My gorgeous little Passion
Flower'. In moments of great affection he may refer
to his wife as a 'good old bag' or a 'dear old faggot' and,
if she should chance to hear the remark, she will blush
with pleasure and feel warm for the rest of the day.

The Gentleman in Bed

By the same token gentlemen are not passionate per-
formers in bed. That is to say they do not wear see-
through pyjamas or spray themselves with mannish
perfumes before diving between the sheets and they
do not study handbooks illustrating a variety of sexual
gymnastics in order to rouse their wives to a frenzy of
passion. Instead they smell faintly of Lifebuoy and prefer to wear flannel next to the skin. Some very dashing
gentlemen have their pyjamas made in their old school
colours while others, less romantically, wear bed-socks
and even night-caps.

One of the hazards of going to bed with a gentleman
is that he often shares it with one or more of his dogs.
Instead of whispering felicitous phrases, his moment
of climax is more likely to be punctuated with cries of
'Down, Brandy, Down! There's a good dog.' Not all
women find this wildly romantic.

[23]

Extramarital Activity

It must not be imagined, because gentlemen do not study the finer points of sexual techniques, that they are uninterested in adventures outside the marriage bed. It is only that, because of their way of life, they do not have the same opportunities for amorous dalliance as do travelling salesmen or company directors with nubile secretaries. Nor is a gentleman capable of the same sort of guile which is employed by the practised philanderer. When he starts to refer to a lady of his own class as 'a demned fine woman' or to someone outside his intimate circle as 'a corker' his wife should pay heed. Anonymous hotel bedrooms or the backs of motor cars are not for him but it is a poor hunt ball which does not provide some convenient shrubbery, and house parties provide excellent excuses for a gentleman to find himself in the wrong bedroom, however familiar he may be with the geography of the house. It is considered important, however, that a gentleman should be back in his room in time for early morning tea, not so much for the sake of his wife but so as not to set a bad example to the servants.

Gentlemen's Wives

Even if, as sometimes happens, a gentleman marries beneath himself, his wife is automatically raised in social status and treated with great respect by trades-men and house servants. Even other gentlemen's wives, whilst they might privately deplore the union, are at pains to admit her to their circle and hope that she will commit some social gaffe which they can retail with gusto to their friends.

All gentlemen's wives, whatever their antecedents, are expected to make themselves available for whatever local activity may require their support, whether it be presiding over the Women's Guild or organizing a stall at a 'Bring and Buy' sale. At the same time they must memorize the names and family circumstances of all those of inferior social status with whom they may come in contact as well as keeping their husbands informed of all anniversaries he is required to recognize in his own family, including her own.

Divorce is generally frowned upon but if it occurs it is generally the husband who elicits the sympathy wherever the blame may lie, unless his wife is very rich in which case he is usually described as a 'bloody fool'.

5
The Gentleman and his Car

A Horse! A Horse! My kingdom for a horse!
KING RICHARD III

THE NATURAL form of locomotion for a gentleman is
the horse. He has never really come to terms with the
motor car but because of the pressures of modern living
he generally owns one or two just the same as everybody
else.

Non-Gent Cars

There are certain cars which it is not done for a gentleman to own. The most non-gent car of all is the Rolls-
Royce. It was not always so. There was a time during
the pioneering days of motoring when it was quite the
done thing. Now that the days of glass partitions and
speaking tubes have given way to cocktail bars and tele-
phones as standard fittings, he has gracefully bowed
out of the market and left the field clear for pop stars
and business tycoons with large expense accounts. If,
however, it happens that he has been left one by an
eccentric aunt there are two conditions under which he
will allow himself to be seen in it. The first condition is
that it should be very old and the second condition that
it should not be very clean. Some gentlemen carry this
second condition further, keeping old sacks in the back
seat and leaving bird messes on the roof where the
chickens have roosted.

Gent Cars

The most acceptable car for a gentleman is an estate
car with a wired-off compartment at the back for the

convenience of his dogs. He does not usually adorn it with dolls dangling from strings in the back window, mock leopard skin cushions or window-stickers announcing that he has been to Llandudno. A few show-off gentlemen, however, indulge in model racehorses, leaping salmon or flying pheasants on the bonnet.

Very often a gentleman's wife will have her own car, particularly if she can afford to buy it herself. Anything that is small and uncomfortable will do. A gentleman will only drive his wife's car in an emergency when he will complain about the steering and the state of the brakes. His wife is never allowed to drive his car unless he is drunk or has gout.

In addition, gentlemen usually have a Land Rover. This is fitted with racks to carry his guns on shooting parties and is loaded with hay bales to serve as a private grandstand at point-to-points.

Not Mechanical

A gentleman never looks under the bonnet of his motor car, for he makes a point of knowing nothing about engines. He would be just as likely to operate on his horse without calling in the vet as he would be to clean a plug without calling in the garage.

Driving Habits

Gentlemen do not drive in their shirtsleeves, lounge behind the wheel with one elbow out of the window or cuddle their lady friends in the front seat. They drive with great decorum and a complete certainty that they are always in the right. They complain constantly about road hogs, women drivers and traffic wardens. They behave in fact as though they were in the hunting field and are capable of some very ungentlemanly language indeed if they are thwarted.

A gentleman never takes his car up to London but

travels by taxi. He always tips the driver exactly one shilling, however far the distance, which results in his opinion that taxi drivers as a class are not nearly so polite as they used to be.

Even mean gentlemen do not travel by bus because they do not understand them. A gentleman of my acquaintance was so impressed by the rumours of the cheapness of bus travel that he determined to give it a trial. Mounting the first bus which came along Piccadilly he was asked by the conductor where he wanted to get off. 'Drive me,' he commanded, 'to 25 Eaton Square.'

Very few gentlemen nowadays employ a man exclusively as a chauffeur. Some, however, enlist the services of a valet or handyman to drive them on such grand occasions as Royal Garden Parties or if they are the sort of gentlemen who have a thing about parking on double yellow lines they have their man drive round the block they are visiting until they emerge, which probably costs as much in petrol as in parking fines.

Finally, the placing of passengers in his car when he and his wife are giving another couple a lift is a matter of protocol which is often overlooked by non-gents, who tend to reserve the front seats of the car for male passengers and the back for females. A gentleman will always seat the lady guest beside him in the front seat and place her husband in the back seat with his own wife. The author does not pretend to know the reasons for this arrangement unless it is designed to stop the ladies indulging in unseemly gossip.

6

The Gentleman at Play

Ye curious carpet knights,
that spend the time in sport and play
HUMPHREY GIFFORD

GENTLEMEN are expected to be good at games while
they are at school. It is greatly to their advantage for, if
they are bad at games, they get their bottoms kicked by
all who are better. After they leave school gentlemen
generally give up organized games with some relief
unless the habit has become so ingrained that they go
on to captain England at something or other.

Gentlemanly Games

Cricket is a very gentlemanly game. So, to a lesser extent,
is Rugby football, referred to by non-gentlemen as
'rugger'. Association football is no longer considered a
gentlemanly game. The practice of footballers kissing
each other after a goal has been scored has lowered the
tone. Kissing in public, even between consenting gentlemen, is not considered to be the done thing. At Rugby,
players do not kiss each other. They confine themselves
to kneeing each other in the groin when the referee
is not looking, which makes it much more gentlemanly.

Gentlemen, Large and Small

Most gentlemen, because of a healthy upbringing, come
in large sizes which is a considerable advantage to them
at school where the law is the survival of the biggest.
There is, however, a limited demand for small gentle-

men who can carve a niche for themselves as scrum halves or coxes or amateur jockeys.

Modesty

Gentlemen who are good at games do not boast about it. Instead they scatter team photographs, oars, cups and caps around their houses and leave it to people to find out for themselves. From time to time they pay visits to the Meccas of their sports like Lord's and Twickenham, wearing the appropriate ties and making loud remarks about the deficiencies of the players.

Golf and Tennis

Games like golf and tennis are not taken seriously by gentlemen although they sometimes play them for the sake of the exercise. They do not have the same approach to these games as lesser mortals. In the case of golf, for example, a gentleman is never seen with one of those vast leather bags, filled with gleaming clubs, some of which are adorned with little woolly hats. Instead he has a thin canvas bag with half a dozen assorted clubs, some of which have wooden shafts which he calls his 'knockers'. With these he hits the ball great distances and has the knack of hacking the ball out of the most appalling rough onto the green. He is altogether a maddening person to play against.

The same applies to tennis, for which he dresses in long once-white trousers, now yellowed with age. In mixed foursomes he plays with great courtesy, serving underhand to the lady even if she is a Wimbledon player. Most of his best shots are played off the wood, which has a demoralizing effect against even the most expert opponents. When he wins he is so sporting about it and goes on so about the luck of the game that most people feel like wringing his neck.

Blood Sports

From his earliest days games take second place in a gentleman's life to blood sports. At his nanny's knee he does not learn sloppy rhymes about Little Jack Horner and Humpty Dumpty, but memorizes recitations which will be useful to him when he is older. Often these rhymes have a strong moral message like:

> Never, never let your gun
> Pointed be at anyone . . .
> All the pheasants ever bred
> Will not make up for one man dead.

As soon as he is old enough he joins a Society for the Preservation of Wild Life and sets about his own life work of keeping down the population of everything from foxes to pheasants.

The keeping down of foxes in particular is felt by most gentlemen to be part of the responsibility of their station in life even if it means making sure that there is always a sufficient supply of foxes to be kept down.

Fair Play for All

It is a characteristic of the gentleman that he always pursues his sport in such a manner as to give his prey the greatest chance of survival. For example he will go to great lengths to see that his pheasants are driven over the guns travelling as fast as possible and at as great an altitude as possible.

In hunting the fox this characteristic is carried to ridiculous lengths involving dressing up in special clothes and setting off on horseback to pursue a pack of foxhounds which may or may not in their turn be pursuing a fox. Gentlemen often break their arms and legs and sometimes their necks but this does not deter them from their sacred duty. If questioned by the uninformed as to why they involve themselves with so

[33]

much ritual they will explain patiently that it all makes it much more enjoyable for the fox.

Salmon Fishing

Fishing it also a very gentlemanly sport but only for trout and salmon. The sort of fishing where you sit on a little stool and watch a float bobbing up and down in the water is not considered gentlemanly and the million or so people who indulge in it are known as 'coarse' fishermen and are quite unacceptable. Gentlemen who own their own fishing frequently let it for large sums of money to gentlemen who do not and catching a rich fishing tenant is often considered just as good a sport as catching your own fish.

Shooting

The highest pinnacle of all gentlemanly sporting activities is shooting. There was a time when there were no gentlemen who did not have their own shooting and for many today it is still considered an indispensable asset.

There was one very gentlemanly gentleman who found himself in the company of a young man with whom he was not very well acquainted. Seeking a subject which he was sure would be common ground, he enquired after his pheasants.

'I am afraid,' the young man told him with some embarrassment, 'that I do not have any.'

'Then it's your own damned fault,' snapped the gentleman. 'Don't feed 'em properly, I'll be bound.'

One of the gentleman's most treasured possessions is his game book in which he keeps a meticulous tally of everything he shoots or catches. This habit was so ingrained with one gentleman that when he decided to take his own life he was careful first to enter himself in the game book under 'various' before pressing the trigger.

Indoor Games

In spite of the strictures earlier in this book about the game of billiards no longer being a gentlemanly way of passing the evening, there are still certain pastimes for which the billiards room is used for after-dinner recreation. (Oddly enough non-gentlemen refer to it as the billiard room as if it were a place where a game called billiard was played.)

On the whole the two main indoor games in which gentlemen are involved are Bridge and Backgammon. Gentlemen are apt to play Bridge as a rather sophisticated form of Whist and are inclined to be ill-informed about Contract Bridge, particularly with regard to the scoring. Notwithstanding, he claims to be an authority on even the most modern conventions and can always find an argument to prove his partner has made a wrong bid if he fails to make his contract – particularly if his partner happens to be his wife.

Backgammon, which is a game which is regarded by many as being of comparatively modern origin, has, in fact, been a gentlemanly game in private houses for many years. The fact that the game is several thousand years old did not deter the gentleman from regarding it as English as foxhunting. His enthusiasm for the game has only declined recently as a result of it being 'discovered' by non-gents who play it in expensive West End gambling clubs for vast sums of money and run vulgar championships in places like Nassau and Antibes, which fill the gentleman who has played the game since childhood for the fun of winning with a feeling that something has gone wrong somewhere.

7
The Gentleman at War

'*C'est magnifique, mais ce n'est pas la guerre*'
MARSCHAL BOSQUET on
'The Charge of the Light Brigade'

IT IS ONE of the stranger anomalies of that formidable military bible, King's Regulations, that one of the commonest charges in bringing an officer before a Court Martial is for 'behaviour unbecoming to an officer and a gentleman'. Long ago, when King's Regulations were first laid down, one would have thought it unneccesary even to the most pedantic legal mind to add the words 'and gentleman', for in those days for a man to be an officer and not a gentleman was unthinkable. Is there some long-forgotten military ghost who, like the farmer in Sir Iain's Foreword, claimed that he was not a gentleman to escape the penalty of his crime? Most unlikely, I should have thought, and more unlikely still that such a defence should prove successful. Before the neccessities of war drew all manner of strange cattle into the commissioned ranks, to be a gentleman was the *sine qua non* of holding a commission.

The last two wars changed all that, and civilians finding themselves wearing the badges of rank of an officer liked to describe themselves with a nice cynicism as 'officers and temporary gentlemen', but by and large they kept up the gentlemanly tradition during their service. As Jorrocks might have said, wearing a pip on the shoulder gave a man 'werry gentlemanly ideas'. Indeed the 'temporary gentlemen' derived not a little enjoyment out of poking fun at the regular officers, many of whom, they felt, were rather apt to stand on their dignity.

There is the story told of two regular officers who, during the Great War, came into collision in a narrow communication trench on a pitch dark night.

'Who the devil are you?' one of them demanded angrily.

'And who might you be?' asked the other.

'I am Major Sir Frank Swinnerton Dyer, Coldstream Guards', retorted the first.

'Oh, are you indeed?' said the second. 'Well, I am Lieutenant-Colonel Lord Henry Seymour, Grenadier Guards. I beat you on all three counts. Get out of the way.'

While, in times of peace, regular officers carry protocol and tradition to what many outsiders might regard as a ridiculous extent, when it comes to going to war they do so with much the same enthusiasm as they show for grouse shooting. The only thing is that they do not treat war quite so seriously.

Most gentlemanly families have a record of service in one capacity or another. The most popular is the Army where a marked preference is shown for the Cavalry or the Guards. The Navy is not so popular largely because you cannot keep your dog, let alone your horse, on board even the largest ships, and the Air Force is altogether too much of a novelty and indeed rather too technical to make a very wide appeal to the traditionalists.

When not involved with the enemy, officers contrive to spend much of their time hunting, shooting and fishing and leave the business of running day-to-day affairs to non-commissioned officers who enjoy that sort of thing. Occasionally they will turn out for manoeuvres, often getting hopelessly lost in the process, before re-

turning to the Mess for a well-earned gin and tonic. It is altogether a very gentlemanly way of life.

On the battlefield an officer is apt immediately to forget all the rules which his men have learned so scrupulously. He dresses rather as if he were out for a Sunday afternoon stroll. He wears his most comfortable clothes and carries a walking stick and a pair of binoculars through which he peers at the enemy with all the interest he might devote to a rare species of bird. It is very difficult for a non-gentleman to behave like a gentleman in battle because non-gents do not have the same belief that all foreigners are bad shots.

Another interesting distinction between officers and other ranks in the field is that whereas other ranks get wounded officers would describe themselves, if, to their surprise, they suffered the same fate, as being 'hit' and they tend to ignore any injuries unless very great. Everyone knows the story of those two very gentlemanly gentleman at the Battle of Waterloo, the Duke of Wellington and his second-in-command, Lord Uxbridge.

'By God, I've lost my leg!' remarked Lord Uxbridge.

'So you have, by God!' remarked his chief as they continued to ride into battle.

There was a similar incident in the last war when a young subaltern had the misfortune to have his reproductive organs removed by a shell which had passed neatly through his legs.

'Good gracious,' he exclaimed, 'whatever will Mummy say?'

While high-ranking officers in all three Services tend to suffer from a certain irascibility, Naval officers in particular have a reputation for tempering their wrath with wit. There was an occasion when an Admiral in his flagship was standing off shore watching a junior officer's attempt to take his craft alongside the harbour wall. Young and inexperienced, he made a thorough mess of the job and so was surprised to see the signal 'Good' hoisted on the flagship. His elation with the thought that he had got away with it was, however, somewhat punctured when, after a considerable delay the word 'God' was added to the message.

Gentlemen who served in the Royal Air Force tended to set themselves apart from the rest if only by the fact that they evolved a vocabulary of their own which made communication with others extremely difficult. Apart from peppering their speech with expressions like 'prang' and 'bang on' they had a tendency to drink vast quantities of beer which constrasted sharply with the Naval devotion to pink gin and the Army's to whisky and soda.

Each service has its own quota of gentlemanly eccentrics and humorists. If I had to select the most outstanding in my own service, the Army, my choice would inevitably fall on David Niven who qualified as a gentleman by joining the Regular Army before forsaking it for the world of greasepaint. Naturally he rejoined the Army during the last war and it was while he was thus engaged that he became involved in one of those many tedious military exercises carried out as rehearsals for the real thing. On this occasion the General commanding our side thought it would be a good idea to try out the merits of homing pigeons as message carriers and rashly selected Niven for the task. Accordingly he found himself ensconced comfortably enough in a pub well behind the 'enemy' lines from which point of vantage he was supposed to send back information about troop movements. However, as the hours slipped past nothing whatever happened and the pigeons cooed away happily in their baskets. Finally, feeling he must justify himself in some way, Niven encoded a message, attached it to a bird's leg and watched it soar away into the distance.

Perhaps surprisingly, it duly arrived and everyone, including the General, clustered round the signals officer while he decoded the message.

It read: 'I have been sent home for pissing in my basket'.

Today peacetime service in certain arms of the service is still regarded as a very gentlemanly business but it somehow lacks the sporting atmosphere of war. In the opinion of most gentlemen there would not be half so much trouble in the world today if we had a little less peace.

8

The Gentleman Abroad

Black men start at Calais

THE ENGLISH gentleman invented abroad.

Edward VII, who was not quite a gentleman but let that pass, was among the first to spread around the rumour that the young ladies of Paris threw off their clothes more readily than their English sisters and the French named a boulevard after him in recognition of his researches on that subject.

Let it be understood that gentlemen do not take holidays in the same way that other people do. That is to say that if they go up to London they do so for a definite and stated purpose, whether it be to buy a suit, see their solicitors or merely to change their watch strap. The fact that they take advantage of the situation to have a few nights out on the tiles is nothing to do with the main business in hand. In this way, if in no other, they resemble businessmen attending a sales convention.

Gentlemen in Europe

The gentleman adventured into Europe not to rest from the onerous business of being a gentleman but to find new outlets for his energy. He had to find something to do between the end of the foxhunting season and the beginning of the shooting season. Thus it came about that he pioneered golf at Le Touquet, gambling at Deauville and boar shooting in the Ardennes. It was because the hard weather made hunting impossible after Christmas that he invented the improbable sport of sliding down Swiss mountains, precariously balanced on two narrow boards. It was because his doctor ordered it that he made it fashionable to sit up to his neck in hot mud at Baden-Baden and to drink the unpleasant-tasting waters of Vichy in the belief that he could then ruin his liver for the rest of the year drinking brandy.

Grateful foreigners

Foreigners have a lot to be grateful to the English gentleman for and, during the last century the French in particular showed their gratitude with their hotels Prince de Galles and Reine Victoria and their Place des Anglais. Admittedly they also christened venereal disease the Pox Britannica and its preventive '*un capot Anglais*', but that is beside the point.

Competition

All that is changed now. The Americans started the rot with their lavish tipping and their eccentric habits like not changing for dinner which has had the effect of both raising the price and lowering the tone so far as the English gentleman is concerned. Of course that is not the end of it all. It was not long before Greek shipping magnates were being bowed over the threshold of the best casinos, moving-picture stars were being given the best suites in hotels and German industrialists were queueing up to be the first into the dining-room of the most expensive restaurants. It all just goes to show that one cannot trust foreigners to know their place any longer.

The Final Thrust

Perhaps the final dagger thrust to the gentleman's flirtation with Europe has been the influx of his own country-men who have deserted the delights of Wigan Pier and

Blackpool illuminations to crowd the beaches of the once fashionable resorts, showing their braces and demanding chips with everything. The English gentleman never smothered himself with sun tan oil or wore dark glasses or flowered shirts and he finds himself a figure of fun being jostled on the promenade in his white ducks and straw boater.

A few gentlemen still go abroad to stay in some beleaguered château in France, to shoot partridges in Spain or to complain that there is no horse-radish sauce with the roast beef in Reid's Hotel in Madeira but now, on the whole, he prefers to stay at home for the Chelsea Flower Show.

There are, however, just a few occupations which still attract the gentleman away from his home shores. It has already been pointed out that it was the English gentleman who invented skiing and, by and large, he has remained an ardent adherent to winter sports. On no account, however, will he be found as a member of a packaged tour taking instructions from some damned fellow in a red jersey. Most gentlemen are very good skiiers indeed, having been taught from a very early age by their fathers or a private tutor. They tend to return year after year to the same resort which their forebears made fashionable, partly because of the respectful treatment they receive from the Swiss hoteliers who, in spite of their reputation for avarice, still prefer to have an English milord as a guest to a German industrialist, and partly because it is in the larger resorts that they can enjoy other aspects of winter sporting which are largelly ignored by the proletariat. Skating is one and curling, a very gentlemanly game, is another. So, too, is bobsleighing which appeals to the liking certain gentlemen have of living dangerously and has so few British adherents who can afford the necessary time or practice that an otherwise idle gentleman has a good chance of making the international team. The peak attraction of all for the gentleman is the Cresta Run which is so designed that the competitior on his sled (correctly *luge*) hurtles down a precipitous and tortuous course at approximately a hundred miles an hour with his nose only inches from the ice. It used to be almost entirely an English form of torture but now, rather to their chagrin, other nations are going in for it, particularly Americans who do rather well at it.

There are still a few gentlemen who preserve the tradition of the 1930s, made fashionable by the Prince of Wales, of spending Easter golfing at Le Touquet and immersing themselves in mud at Baden-Baden but, of late, there has developed an even more gentlemanly activity abroad – visiting old battlefields. Expeditions are still being fitted out for incredibly old gentlemen of Great War vintage to visit the once blood-soaked beaches of Gallipoli in the Dardanelles, but the battlefields of the last war all over Europe have an increasing annual quota of bristly moustached ex-officers with walking sticks, binoculars and map cases pointing out to each other the exact spot where 'poor old Bertie caught his' or where 'we blew up that damned Kraut tank'.

Like the common tripper who boasts of his exploits in his Spanish resort for the rest of the year, visiting battlefields provides the gentleman with a party monologue for many a dinner party through the long winter months ahead.

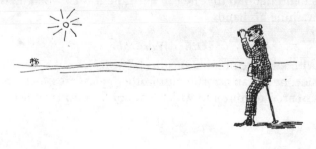

9

The Gentleman and his Wardrobe

Fine clothes are good only as they supply the
want of other means of procuring respect
DR JOHNSON

NOTHING gives away a man's standing as a gentleman
so much as his clothes.

His Suits

Those people who have a suit for every day of the week
and even, one is reluctantly led to believe, more ex-
pansive wardrobes, are parvenus of the worst sort. A
gentleman generally has two suits. There is one for
formal occasions like funerals and another for less
formal occasions like going up to London. They are
made by one of a select band of exclusive tailors and
last him many years until his wife judges they are too
threadbare. Then they are either handed down to the
gardener or given to a good cause like the Distressed
Gentlefolk's Aid Association. By this time, with any
luck, his tailor has been paid and he buys two more.
The criterion of a gentleman's suit is that it should fit
well round the shoulders and that the cuff buttons
should undo so that he can turn them back when he is
washing his hands.

Other Wardrobe

Although the number of suits he owns is on the meagre
side, he has an assortment of other garments which are
essential to him and which seldom find a place in the

wardrobes of others. He has, for example, a jacket for every occasion. If he is a hunting gentleman he will have a hunting jacket. He will also have a hacking jacket, a shooting jacket and a gardening jacket which no self-respecting gardener would ever be seen in and they invariably have horn or leather buttons, several of which will be missing. He has a dinner jacket with trousers to match which must under no circumstances be called a 'dinner suit'. If he has evening tails he apologizes for them, saying that they belonged to his grandfather, which is almost certainly true. A gentleman will sometimes wear a white waistcoat with his dinner jacket, particularly if he cannot find a black one and not mind being whispered about by non-gents, for it is perfectly permissible. He will not, however, wear a black waistcoat with tails, which is the prerogative of hotel waiters. A gentleman will also have a morning coat which he wears with rather dashing light-coloured trousers totally unlike those dark striped ones which are rented out by dress-hire firms.

Good Tailors

Gentlemen may wear their suits until they are thread bare but they do so with considerable panache and it is evident to the most uncritical eye that they have been built by a good tailor. As one gentleman remarked about the members of a club which he considered socially inferior to his own, 'They are quite a decent lot of chaps. It is only a pity that they all seem to make their own trousers . . .'

There are, too, certain little touches to the way a gentleman dresses which sets him apart from the less socially elevated. For example, the flaps on his jacket pockets are always tucked into the pocket itself and he always wears the bottom button of his waistcoat undone. This latter idiosyncracy has its origins in the days when Edward VII was the leader of Society. Nicknamed 'Tum-Tum' because of his great bulk he always had difficulty in doing up the bottom button and when eventually he gave up trying, other gentlemen politely followed suit.

The Sports Jacket

No gentleman ever has a garment which is popularly called a sports jacket. Nor does he ever wear a blazer with a badge on the pocket. The only exception to gentlemen not wearing blazers is at Henley when they turn out in creations they have had since their rowing days and which would make a stage comedian look ridiculous.

His Shoes

A gentleman always has well polished shoes which are generally hand-made and last a lifetime. They are polished with ox-blood which is a similar eccentricity to washing his riding breeches in urine. On less formal occasions he wears gum boots which are usually green and have a little strap to tighten them below the knee.

Shirts and Underwear

Shirts are always bought in Jermyn Street, an extravagance which is made to pay off by dint of having the cuffs and collars turned when they get worn, which gives them many years of life. This is not to say that a gentleman is necessarily mean but he dislikes waste where the efforts of his wife or servants can avoid it. By contrast with the exclusivity of Jermyn Street he always buys his underwear at Marks & Spencer and always tells his friends about it as an indication that he is democratic about his clothes. In fact, a lot of time is taken up at cocktail parties by gentlemen telling each other where they buy their underwear.

Accessories

A gentleman carries the minimum of accessories. Those who go around with what is known as the Cartier set – gold lighters, gold cigarette cases, watches with crocodile straps and so on are put down as bookmakers or confidence tricksters. A gentleman carries Swan Vestas matches instead of a lighter, except possibly a rather roughly-made lighter fitted with a special windshield which enables him to light it in a howling gale on a grouse moor or in the middle of a salmon river. If he has a cigarette case it is usually a heavy silver affair which he has inherited but does not often carry as it spoils the cut of his suit. His only adornment is a pair of modest crested cuff-links, although in full plumage for the races at Ascot he may sport a tie-pin. There are also still gentlemen who appear on certain occasions wearing a watch chain. The practice has grown less frequent since the death of Sir Winston Churchill who *always* wore a watch chain of a design which most gentlemen would have considered more appropriate to a civic dignitary who had made his money out of hosiery. But then there were many gentlemen who did not consider Churchill to be quite a gentleman. A gentleman always wears his handkerchief tucked in his sleeve – never carefully arranged in his top pocket – an art which is as difficult to acquire as tying a bow tie. It has been brought to my notice that no less an authority on the upper classes than Nancy Mitford, who should know better, declares that gentlemen should wear their handkerchiefs in their top pocket. This is to subscribe to the middle-class practice of having one carefully arranged handkerchief in the top pocket and another somewhere else on the person. This principle of 'one for show and one for blow' is as non-U as a lady who carries her handkerchief tucked in the elastic of her knickers.

A gentleman is particular about having a good watch and takes great pride in its time-keeping qualities. One gentleman to whom it was pointed out that his watch had stopped, exploded: 'That is impossible! My man always winds it before he puts it on me in the morning.'

In the country he wears a flat hat in a manner which is quite different from the flat hats worn by the working classes and, whatever the weather, he carries a walking stick. In the town he may carry a carefully rolled umbrella but he never thinks of opening it. Many gentlemen have never unrolled their umbrellas since they bought them. He only wears a bowler hat at funerals and point-to-points.

The Old School Tie

One of the most distinctive items of a gentleman's wardrobe is his collection of ties. They are always of a quiet design with the exception of the MCC tie if he happens to have been a cricketer. This is the most vulgar of all club ties and he wears it with a certain amount of embarrassment when the Test Matches are on. He always has a black tie to wear on Armistice Day and there is, of course, his regimental tie and his old school tie. Etonians wear their school tie much more frequently and ostentatiously than gentlemen who went to other schools. There is the story of the socially ambitious young man who had not been to Eton, but wished he had, who spotted a man selling matches in the street wearing the coveted tie. To show off his knowledge to his girl friend he stopped and demanded: 'What the devil do you mean by wearing an Old Etonian tie?' 'Because,' replied the other equally, 'I cannot afford to buy a new one.'

Although in the course of his life a gentleman is apt to collect a large number of club and other institutional ties, it is not really done to wear them except when attending the function to which they are appropriate. Bow ties largely went out of fashion with the death of Sir Winston Churchill, just as buttonholes declined in popularity after the Great Greenfly plague.

The Casual Look

In short, a gentleman looks well-dressed and has an indefinable distinction even in his oldest clothes. At home he is quite likely to wear a pullover which has a hole in the front and he patches his jackets with leather when they become frayed at the cuffs or out at the elbow – a characteristic which is emulated by many non-gents who sew leather patches onto new jackets in the vain hope that they will be mistaken for what they are not.

The knack gentlemen have of dressing badly and getting away with it is best illustrated by the story of the gentleman who was accosted by a friend walking along Piccadilly in clothes which were well below the best sartorial standards.

'It does not matter how I dress in London,' he claimed. 'Nobody here knows me.'

Later the same friend visited him in the country where his clothes were no better.

'It does not matter how I dress here', he said, 'Everybody knows me.'

10
The Gentleman and his Relationships

> O let us love our occupations
> Bless the squire and his relations
> Live upon our daily rations
> And always know our proper stations
> CHARLES DICKENS

A GENTLEMAN'S relationship with his fellow beings in an extremely complex matter which outsiders often find difficult to understand. The result is that he gives offence when he is trying to be polite and, when he is being intentionally rude, it often passes over his victim's head.

The Prefix

A great deal of misunderstanding revolves around the use or omission of the prefix 'Mister'. For gentlemen to address a person by his surname only is often taken as a slight. However, it is a compliment and a form of address which is reserved for (a) those of his own class whom he does not know intimately but who meet with his approval, and (b) those of the lower classes who are concerned with his personal comfort and whom he holds in high esteem. This includes his personal servant, the barman at the club, his hairdresser and doormen at the more exclusive hotels.

The prefix 'Mister' is only used with those whom he wishes to keep at arm's length, like Government officials, tradesmen to whom he owes money or politicians with whose politics he does not agree. If he uses it to someone to whom he has been introduced socially it is a positive affront.

Names and Titles

By the same token the gentleman is always very careful to get a name right unless he has reason to dislike somebody, in which case he is at great pains to get the name wrong. Thus Mr Jones becomes Mr Smith, Mr White becomes Mr Black and Mr Bottomleigh becomes Mr Bumley.

Gentlemen are scrupulous in the matter of titles. No matter how well he may know a Peer of the Realm he will always refer to him formally when mentioning his name to a third party who does not have the advantage of knowing him. This is in sharp contrast to the name-dropper who tries to impress his friends with his intimacy with the aristocracy by using their first names whether he knows them or not. In their efforts to prove the closeness of their friendships social climbers often go too far. The Duke of Devonshire, for example, is seldom addressed as 'Andy' or the Duke of Buccleuch as 'Jack'. Nor is the outsider to know that the 10th Earl Montmorency, 13th Viscount, 15th Baron and 21st Baronet, traditional Lord High Keeper of The Queen's Turtle Doves, is invariable known to his intimates as 'Stinker'.

These are deliberate traps set by gentlemen in the path of the unwary, for if there is one thing that gentlemen wish to avoid at all costs it is to be tricked into intimacy with someone outside their own circle. They even like to select those they wish to avoid from among those social equals. As one of them put it: 'If I am going to be bored, I would rather be bored by a Lord.'

Private Drinkers

It is for this same reason that gentlemen do not drink in public unless they are far from their home ground. The habit of dropping into the local on a Sunday morning, so much the fashion nowadays among the bourgeoisie, is just not done. If by chance he has called in for a packet of cigarettes and is offered a drink by one of the regulars, however, he will accept it graciously and if there are any more like-minded persons he will accept drinks from them also, for it would be impolite to refuse. He will then leave without returning the compliment, for it is his rule only to offer people drinks in the privacy of his own home. The fact that this sometimes causes him to be referred to as a 'miserable old bastard' does not worry him in the slightest.

The Family

The gentleman's relationship with his own family is much less complicated. After the first passionate nights he preserves towards his wife an attitude of kindly patronage. He encourages her to seek her pleasures in such diverse activities as have already been mentioned as appropriate to her position. He realizes that she may wish to break out from time to time in such excesses as a Bridge afternoon or a ladies' four at tennis, and he does not stand in her way. On occasions he will even let her have the run of the drawing-room for such purposes as inviting the vicar's wife to tea and he will obligingly make himself scarce so as not to cramp her style.

He regards his children in their earliest years as entirely the concern of the female members of the household. When they get older, however, he takes an increasing interest in them and even shows a certain amount of reserved affection. He allows them to be displayed on occasions to his friends and in time learns to distinguish the girls from the boys. (When reminded by his wife of an impending birthday he will buy the girls little presents for their ponies and the boys gifts like sharp knives and catapults.)

Naturally enough he takes a greater interest in the upbringing of the boys than the girls, even having them in for an interview in his study from time to time to test their knowledge on such vital topics as the nesting habits of the Capercailzie.

When they go to school he reads their reports with the greatest care, taking great pride in their achievements at games but regarding them with the deepest suspicion should they come more than halfway up in their class order. A gentleman's children are expected to conform in all things and academic brilliance is not an acceptable deviation from the normal. The fact that Lord Byron showed promise as a poet was due to the fact that he was brought up by his nurse.

His Dogs

A gentleman's deepest affection is, however, reserved for his dogs. They are always of the sporting variety and usually Black Labradors. Their degree of intimacy with

their master depends on their age. Young dogs are kept in outdoor kennels and trained to be obedient when out shooting. If they should be so rash as to follow their natural instincts and chase a rabbit they are beaten to within an inch of their lives but they are readily forgiven and returned to favour. A gentleman loves his dogs more and more the older they get. In this he resembles the Chinese, who have the same attitude of veneration for old age. In the case of a gentleman the worship of his dog reaches its apotheosis when they are so old and cantankerous that they are deaf and blind and smell of blocked drains. Then they enjoy the best chair in the drawing room, from which point of vantage they enjoy their last remaining pleasure of biting anyone who comes near them.

It is generally considered ungentlemanly to own dogs which bark or, worse still, snarl at visitors. One very ladylike friend of mine holds firmly to this rule for all dogs except her own – she has six Alsatians!

11

The Gentleman and the Church

The Parson knows enough who knows a Duke
WILLIAM COWPER

THE GENTLEMAN'S attitude towards the church is paternalistic. He treats the vicar with friendly condescension, referring to him as 'Vicar' and his wife as 'Mrs Vicar'. He asks them up for occasional glasses of sherry and enquires about the old age pensioners, the new babies and the progress of the roof restoration fund.

Going to Church

He goes to church at regular intervals with his wife and children. This is not because he feels in need of spiritual guidance but to set a good example to those whose chance of entering the Kingdom of Heaven is less certain. He waits until the rest of the congregation are seated before ushering his family down the aisle to take their place in the front pew which is cordoned off for his special use. From this point of vantage he turns round to glare at anyone who arrives after him.

A gentleman sings hymns with great enthusiasm, frequently putting off the choir with his rendering in 'basso profundo'. His favourite hymns are 'Onward, Christian Soldiers', 'Fight the Good Fight' and 'For Those in Peril on the Sea'. He likes hymns where he can show off by not looking at the words in the hymnbook which frequently results in his getting them wrong. During prayers he makes a great show of reverence but if they are unduly prolonged he is apt to interrupt with a loud 'Amen' and sit back in his seat which has the effect of drying up all but the most determined of vicars. When he reads the lesson he does so with great gusto with particular emphasis on those parts of the Old Testament which refer to fornicators and sinners.

Church Affairs

On the whole gentlemen do not like to become too closely involved in church affairs. They do, however, encourage their wives to play a full part in the life of the community. Gentlemen's wives sit on committees, are Presidents of almost everything and open fêtes at the drop of a flowered hat. Gentlemen confine their activity to giving a box of apples to the Harvest Festival and sending the vicar a bottle of port for Christmas.

By and large gentlemen believe in God because, by and large, they are confident that God believes in them.

12

The Gentleman and his Domestic Habits

You Gentlemen of England who live at home at ease
MARTIN PARKER

GENTLEMEN do not, unless it cannot be avoided, eat out in restaurants. The exceptions to this rule are a few exclusive hotels in the West End of London where they can, at great expense, get such delicacies as Brown Windsor, a thin tasteless soup traditionally served by the Royal Family, and milk puddings like rice and sago which are a relic of their nursery days. They do not like food which has been 'messed about with'. Continental cooking gives them diarrhoea.

Home Food

At home they like to eat poultry, fish or game which they themselves have reared, caught or shot. In the old days salmon and venison appeared so regularly on the menus of Scottish households that the servants, who were stuck with the same fare as their masters, rebelled and stipulated that they should not be required to eat such delicacies more than twice a week. Now all the salmon is put on fast trains to London, venison is sent to Germany and the servants are lucky if they get a look in at the tinned Snoek.

If a gentleman has a cook or his wife has a penchant for cooking they are allowed to run the whole gamut of the culinary arts in such matters as whether the pheasant should be served with bread sauce or fried breadcrumbs. If there are guests for dinner, extravagances such as savouries are sometimes permitted. Gentlemen are very fond of savouries. If there are any left over they are apt to shovel them all onto their own plates in spite of agonized signals from their wives. Then they want to know why the guests are not having any more and they have to pretend that they do not want any more.

Vulgarities

There are certain objects which are never seen on a gentleman's dining table – fish forks and knives for example, which are regarded as a Victorian vulgarity except by those whose fortunes were made in Victorian times. Another are napkin rings. I remember a gentleman asking to be enlightened as to the use of napkin rings. It was explained to him that some people rolled up their napkins and placed them inside the ring to be kept ready for the next meal. 'Good God!' he exploded, 'D'ye mean to tell me they use the same napkin for two meals running!'

Wine Drinking

Gentlemen are very concerned about maintaining a good cellar and by and large know what they are talking

about when dealing with their wine merchants. Some wealthy gentlemen even still preserve the tradition of laying down a pipe of port to be enjoyed by their sons when they come of age.

At the same time gentlemen are singularly free from wine snobbery. They acquire any reasonable plonk for their day-to-day requirements and, if it so happens that they have a preference for, say, red wine, they will drink it with anything, regardless of the vapourings of professional wine writers about white wine with fish and so on.

Cigar Smoking

Most gentlemen smoke cigars but it is a practice which has its pitfalls. Originally the band was put around the cigar by the manufacturer to protect the white gloves worn by gentlemen from nicotine stains. With the falling out of fashion of white gloves the band was often removed, particularly by those who liked to get their money's worth and smoke the thing to the very end. Now only the most traditionally minded and gentlemanly of gentlemen and ostentatious bookmakers do not remove the band. Thus, nowadays, not to do so is to be taken by the observer to being either very upper class or a bookmaker. Most fear that the wrong conclusion will be reached and remove the band.

Punctuality

One of the characteristics of a gentleman is that he is punctual to a fault. He sits down to his meals exactly at the appointed hour and expects to be served even if there has been a power cut or the cook has run off with the second footman. This rule also applies to guests staying the night. If they are not downstairs by the time breakfast is served they have to put up with cold coffee and congealed bacon and eggs.

The same punctuality rules his drinking habits. He pours his first drink at the same hour every day and drinks precisely his quota. If it is his custom to get drunk after dinner, he does so every night whether he is in his own house or somebody else's. This practice can cause consternation if he is so rash as to move outside his own circle. In fact, a gentleman seldom dines out with any but his closest friends, any more than he has a casual acquaintance to dinner in his own house. Acquaintances are asked to drinks only, when they are offered the alternative of dry sherry or gin and tonic without ice.

Dinner Parties

On the whole, gentlemen give dinner parties in order to fraternize with other gentlemen. It is considered polite to make conversation with ladies who are seated next to you at table but that is as far as communication between the sexes is allowed to go. After dinner the ladies 'must' retire to the drawing room for their coffee while the gentlemen settle down to the port and brandy. Contrary to general belief, they do not tell each other dubious stories when they are left together. This is not from any form of prudishness but because they have not heard any new stories since they left school, where they used to giggle over them in the latrines. Everyone knows that the only new stories originate in the Stock Exchange and are repeated by stockbrokers to their cronies in the golf club. Gentlemen are not stockbrokers and do not play golf often. (See Chapter 6)

The final ritual for gentlemen before they rejoin the ladies is for their host to lead them outside to urinate in the garden. The resultant patches of dead grass on the lawn are put down to wireworm and the blighted roses are blamed on the damned greenfly.

13

The Gentleman and his Money

Hey Willow waly O!
Money I despise it
W. S. GILBERT

IT HAS already been remarked that gentlemen do not work but this is only partly true, for there are certain occupations in which a gentleman can indulge. It is one of the conditions, however, that whatever he undertakes should have little chance of showing a satisfactory financial return.

Gentlemanly jobs

A good example of a gentlemanly occupation is chicken farming, which a great number of gentlemen have taken up with enthusiasm at some stage in their lives. They work at it with great energy, cleaning out the henhouses themselves and keeping a scrupulous account of their earnings and outgoings. Carried away by the thought of the substantial profits they are going to make and priding themselves on their scientific approach, they invest in every piece of new equipment or type of feeding stuff which comes on the market. It is usually several years before they accept the fact that they have been making a heavy annual loss. They then give it up and go in for pheasant rearing or mink farming or mushroom growing on the same optimistic basis.

Sons and daughters

Gentlemen's sons, while waiting to inherit from their fathers and so becoming fully-fledged gentlemen themselves, often spend a number of years in one of the Services and especially the Army, which used to be a particularly gentlemanly occupation. In recent years, however, the pay in the Army has become so high that, except in very smart regiments, it is no longer absolutely necessary to have a private income and its popularity as a gentlemanly pastime has decreased as a result.

In this permissive age a few gentlemen's sons are now venturing into such marginal occupations as merchant banking or playing the drums in a pop group but on the whole it is their sisters who show the greater activity in the market place. They open boutiques and antique shops and little restaurants in which they compete with each other with commendable singlemindedness for the custom of each other's friends.

Money is vulgar

One of the root causes of the gentleman's hang-up about making money is that it is one of the things he has always been brought up to believe that it is vulgar to mention. The other is sex. Like sex, however, it is never very far from his thoughts. This shows through, apart from the time when he complains about the price of cartridges or whisky, when other people's money is discussed. To his way of thinking, a gentleman who inherits money or marries it is a very different proposition to the fellow who has had the temerity to make his own. In his view gentlemen fall into one of three financial categories.

'Well off': any gentleman with large estates and several million pounds.

'Comfortably off': any gentleman who would regard winning the football pools with indifference.

'As poor as a church mouse': any gentleman who is down to his last butler and can only just afford to send his sons to Eton.

[65]

By contrast any self-made man is described as 'stinking rich' or 'filthy rich' regardless of the size of his fortune. The fact is that to make money is a very ungentlemanly activity indeed.

14

How to be a Gentleman

A King may make a nobleman but he cannot
make a gentleman

EDMUND BURKE

EVEN IN a book as deeply researched as this one it is
only possible to describe the habits of a gentleman in
the most general terms. It may not be inappropriate,
therefore, to include here a few notes for the guidance
of those who aspire to join their ranks.

Right thinking

It is first of all necessary to acquire the right 'attitude
of mind'. This entails the acceptance of the belief that
gentlemen are a race apart, above the run of ordinary
mortals. One cannot take a day off, for being a gentleman is a full-time occupation, nor can one accept some
of the dogmas and ignore others. Oscar Wilde, who described foxhunting as 'the unspeakable in full pursuit
of the uneatable', showed that he definitely did not
have the right attitude of mind and paid the penalty for
it. Being a gentleman is not a thing to be made a mock
of.

Servants

Of all a gentleman's servants the ones who are allowed
the greatest latitude in familiarity and whom he holds
in the greatest respect are his keeper or ghillie. Keepers
in particular have an unusual licence to abuse his guests
if their performance does not come up to his exacting

standards or to insist in conducting a game drive the way he wants to, even if his master disagrees.

They are in a class of their own as family retainers and the guest would be well advised to remember it.

There was the ghillie who took a guest out salmon fishing on an exceptionally wet day. The guest flogged the river for hours on end and took frequent recourse to the comfort of a bottle of whisky but never offered a dram to his patient companion. Finally, trying to light his pipe, he found his matchbox wet and nowhere dry enough to strike a match.

'Isn't there a single dry spot on the whole of this goddam river?' he complained angrily.

'You could try the back of my throat,' suggested the ghillie poker-faced.

No gentleman would have put himself in the position of deserving such a rebuke.

Speech

Aspiring gentlemen must be very careful about their mode of speech. This has nothing to do with accent for many gentlemen have very strange accents indeed, derived from an upbringing largely spent in the stable-yard. It is not the accent, it is the words you use which matter. Nancy Mitford, with all her goings on about U and non-U, fairly put the cat among the pigeons. Quite ordinary people suddenly started talking about chimney-pieces while gentlemen continued to call them mantel-shelves which only added confusion to an already confusing situation. There are, however, certain expressions which gentlemen never use and are traps for the unwary.

In addressing each other, for example, they never use familiarities like 'old boy', 'old fellow', or 'old chap'.

They do not have their 'dinner' in the middle of the day, they do not use 'serviettes' and their wives do not wear 'costumes'. Most important of all, gentlemen never go to the 'toilet'. Anything from the 'lavatory' to the 'thunder box' will do, but never the 'toilet' or even 'the littlest room'.

Nor do gentlemen adopt modern catch phrases like 'ongoing situation' or 'in no way'.

A gentleman's speech is short to the point of brusqueness so that even when he is being at his most polite he is apt to give the impression that he is issuing orders to his troops. He does not use long words largely because he does not know any. He is also apt to take things up wrong, particularly if he wants to. One Scottish gentleman, on being asked by a coy lady, 'Do tell me, is there anything worn under your kilt?' replied stiffly, 'Madam, to the best of my knowledge everything under my kilt is in perfect working order.'

Neatness

However eccentric a gentleman may be in matters of dress, he always has well brushed hair, clean finger nails and perfectly polished shoes. To fall short on these essentials is to suggest he has been involved in some activity not becoming his status.

Train travel

When a gentleman travels by train he always introduces himself to the engine driver before setting out on his journey and thanks him afterwards if he considers he has driven his train well. This springs from a belief that he still holds shares in the railway and that all staff are his personal servants.

This attitude has its origins in the fact that when the railways were first built it was the landowners who gave permission for them to cross their land which some did gracefully enough and others only after hard bargaining.

An example was the late 5th Earl of Lonsdale who laid it down as one condition that they should provide him with his own railway station. Whenever he himself travelled by train from London to his northern estates he usually had with him as many as half a dozen dogs, for each of whom he would book a first-class sleeper.

On one occasion the railway authorities had the temerity to write to say that one of the passengers had been disturbed by one of his Lordship's dogs barking.

Furiously he wrote back that his dogs travelled at his own express orders and if there were any further complaints from the public he would close his station. The railway company withdrew their complaint with an abject apology.

In the field

There are many more details of gentlemanly behaviour which can be easily enough assimilated by the conscientious student. He will still not, however, pass muster as a gentleman until he has mastered the art of being a gentleman in the field. In the hunting field this is relatively simple, providing he remembers which side to mount his horse and takes care not to fall off on the other side. He must also realize that once he is in the saddle he must be as rude as possible to anyone who crosses his path. One quasi-gentleman, when he was asked by the Master what the devil he thought he was doing out hunting, was naïve enough to reply that he only came out for the fresh air and exercise. 'In that case you had better go home and bugger yourself with a pair of bellows,' thundered the Master, riding off in pursuit of another victim for his scorn.

At sea

Gentlemen who go sailing suffer from much the same malady. However mild they may be on 'terra firma', as soon as they step aboard they drive their crews to the point of mutiny with a flow of language which would make Captain Bligh sound like an officer in the Salvation Army.

The truth is that what people will obstinately refer to as 'messing about in boats' is not really very gentlemanly. There are of course a lot of gentlemen who belong to exclusive clubs like the Royal Yacht Squadron and the Royal Corinthian and there were of course the days when the Royal Yacht Squadron blackballed Edward VII's (a keen sailor) friend, the millionaire Sir Thomas Lipton because he was a grocer. It still remains an extremely exclusive club but those were the days when gentlemen had enormous, luxurious yachts on which they gave grand parties on occasions like the Review of the Fleet or as a comfortable base when they visited the South of France. To have a luxury yacht then had much the same *cachet* as owning a grouse moor.

Now, alas, much of the glory has departed. The old wooden sailing boats which the gentry used to race against each other have been replaced with plastic monstrosities with immensely powerful engines and the spirit of professionalism has ousted the amateur.

There is, however, at least one gentlemanly characteristic in which the gentleman can hold his own amidst the new rich. Whenever sailing men meet there is an air of conviviality and corks are pulled on a scale of which the most sociable of eighteenth-century clubmen would have thoroughly approved.

Shooting

An activity which should be approached with much greater caution than any of the above is shooting. It is not enough to go to the finest gunmakers, dress in the most correct clothes and equip oneself with all the impedimenta from dog whistles to shooting sticks. It is also necessary to know what one is shooting at. There are quite a few objects which it is not done to shoot. These, in order of importance, are one's host, one's host's dog, one's fellow guests' dogs and one's fellow guests. Keepers and beaters come further down the list but they are still not regarded as fair game.

Almost as important as not shooting what one is not supposed to, is to shoot what one is supposed to. At the end of each drive there comes the moment of truth when the head keeper arrives to ask you what birds there are to pick up. If there aren't any after the beaters have walked five miles to drive them over your gun, it is unlikely that you will be the most popular boy in the class or the one most likely to be asked again. Beginners are advised to arrive at their first shoot with the inside pockets of their shooting jackets (which are made specially large for the purpose) filled with dead birds which they have had the foresight to buy at the game dealers and which they can scatter around for the dogs to find. It is, of course, important not to scatter around grouse in the middle of a pheasant shoot and vice versa.

The correct conversation also plays a very important part in establishing one's reputation as a sportsman. It is as well for the aspirant gentleman to equip himself with a few suitable place names to drop around. A brief study of the works of romantic lady novelists is helpful. Names like Enderby, Chevenings or High Tor sound just about right. An opening gambit like 'When I was shooting with old Charles at Chevenings last

week . . .' is a hard one to counter and opens up all sorts of opportunities for a modest recital of your own prowess. Controlled self-deprecation is also a good line. 'I never shoot with two guns now. Not as quick as I used to be y'know'. Or 'Missed three birds running the other day. Made me feel an awful ass' leaves the listener in no doubt that you are one hell of a performer.

In spite of the fact that the young gentleman learns the rules of safety when out shooting from his very tenderest years, accidents will and do happen. It is perhaps only fair to add that these are usually as a result of carelessness by someone who has made enough money to take up the sport late in life. Whoever is the offender, however, the unwritten law is that he leaves the party immediately and if the accident is at all serious, he is not expected to shoot again. By the same token the name of the culprit is never disclosed to even one's closest friends.

This standard etiquette is not always observed by visitors from overseas. At a recent shoot held by an American syndicate one of the guns managed to achieve the quite remarkable feat at the end of one drive of 'peppering' no less than eight beaters with one barrel. Not only was he not sent home but he was asked to shoot again the next day. It was only the number of the beaters which had declined.

Stalking

Another gentlemanly sport where the aspirant would be well advised to employ a little gamesmanship is stag shooting. This entails crawling behind a ghillie up precipitous hillsides in the hope of getting near enough to the stag for a shot. The rule for the inexperienced here is never to put yourself in a position when you have 'to let off your rifle'. If you cannot contrive to send a loose rock rolling down the hillside or inadvertently show your rump above the skyline when the ghillie isn't looking, but the stag is, you must pretend that you have a fly in your eye or, in desperation, omit to load your rifle. The point is that if you wound the beast, which is likely, you are in duty bound to follow it to the end which means a few hours dragging yourself up hill and down dale when your more fortunate companions are enjoying whisky and soda round their own firesides. It is far better to get home early and complain loudly about your bad luck.

Royal Garden Parties

If the aspirant gentleman plays his cards right, the time will come sooner or later when he will be invited to a Royal Garden Party. This is the high point in his career and he must make the most of it without letting it be known that he is in the least bit flattered. It is not done, for example, to carry the card in one's pocket and show it to everyone one meets. It must be placed on the mantelpiece. Even gentlemen indulge in the rather vulgar habit of displaying their invitations on the mantelpiece (or chimneypiece as Miss Mitford prefers it), some even going so far as to write 'accepted' or 'refused' in the top corner as if they had so many invitations that they have to remind themselves which ones they have agreed to attend. It is good tactics to ask as many people in for drinks as possible while the Royal invitation is on display so as to gain maximum exposure.

It is also another opportunity for carefully contrived conversational gambits, although one must be careful to play the thing down: 'Damned nuisance these affairs in the middle of the grouse shooting but my wife likes going to them' or 'My morning coat is getting a bit frayed at the cuffs but I'm damned if I'm going to get a new one' are both good throw-away lines which imply a suitable weariness at being asked so often.

Because nowadays Royal Garden Parties are democratic affairs, it is necessary to strike just the right note of 'savoir-faire'. It is all too easy to get put in the wrong category by the rubbernecks standing round the Palace gates. As Hilaire Belloc put it

> The rich arrived in pairs
> And also in Rolls-Royces;
> They talked of their affairs
> In loud and strident voices.
>
> The poor arrived in Fords,
> Whose features they resembled,
> They laughed to see so many Lords
> And Ladies all assembled.
>
> The people in between
> Look underdone and harassed,
> And out of place and mean
> And horribly embarrassed.

The gentleman of course comes in none of these categories for he is a race apart. He arrives in his own car preferably with a chauffeur sitting beside him and his ladies in the back seat and he walks into the Palace, looking neither to right nor left, as if he had been there many times before.

During the party he makes knowledgeable remarks to anyone standing near him like: 'I see they have made a lot of changes in the herbaceous border', or 'I always think the Palace Gardens look at their best at this time of year'. It is not done to seek out The Queen to shake her hand but it is as well to be prepared for her sudden appearance. It is a useful tip never to accept the rather sticky meringues which are frequently served at Royal Garden Parties. The day after a garden party the gardeners frequently find meringues with false teeth still stuck in them where they had been hurriedly disposed of behind a rose bush at the approach of Her Majesty.

For many months after the garden party is over it is possible to impress on new acquaintances that one has been there. They might be flattered when you say: 'Didn't we meet at Buckingham Palace in the summer?'

These are only a few pointers to guide the faltering footsteps of those who feel that the grass is greener over the fence. It is only to be hoped that when you get there that you don't sit down on a cowpat.

Good luck.

As the gentleman said – you're going to need it.